FIELD TRIPS

The Police Station

Stuart A. Kallen
ABDO & Daughters

Published by Abdo & Daughters, 4940 Viking Drive, Suite 622, Edina, Minnesota 55435.

Copyright © 1997 by Abdo Consulting Group, Inc., Pentagon Tower, P.O. Box 36036, Minneapolis, Minnesota 55435 USA. International copyrights reserved in all countries. No part of this book may be reproduced in any form without written permission from the publisher.

Printed in the United States.

Cover and Interior Photo credits: Peter Arnold, Inc.
                                    Archive Photos
                                    Wide World Photos
Illustration: Ben Dann Lander
Edited by Julie Berg

Library of Congress Cataloging-in-Publication Data

Kallen, Stuart A., 1955-
The police station / Stuart A. Kallen.
p. cm. — (Field trips)
Includes index.
Summary: Describes the work done by various people at a police station.
ISBN 1-56239-708-7
1. Police—Juvenile literature. 2. Police stations—Juvenile literature. [1. Police. 2. Police stations.]
I. Title. II. Series.
HV7922.K35 1997
363.2—dc20
                                           96-20405
                                           CIP
                                           AC

Contents

Emergency!

Sirens wail and lights flash! There's an emergency and the police are on the way. If there's trouble, the police will soon be there to stop it. Any time of day or night, we depend on the police to keep our streets safe.

Every day police officers report to work at the police station. There they get their orders and go to work protecting you and your community.

**Opposite page:
Police cars with their sirens
wailing and lights flashing.**

The Police Station

Almost every city and town has a police station. Big cities have many police stations. If you visit a police station you will meet men and women in uniforms. They are police officers.

You will see a lot of busy people when you walk into a police station. Officers are talking on telephones. People are sitting on benches. Some people are there to report crimes. Some people are there because they committed crimes. **Suspects** are fingerprinted and booked at the police station.

Police officers enforce laws made by governments. Governments from the city, the state, and the county pass laws. Police officers are sworn to uphold those laws.

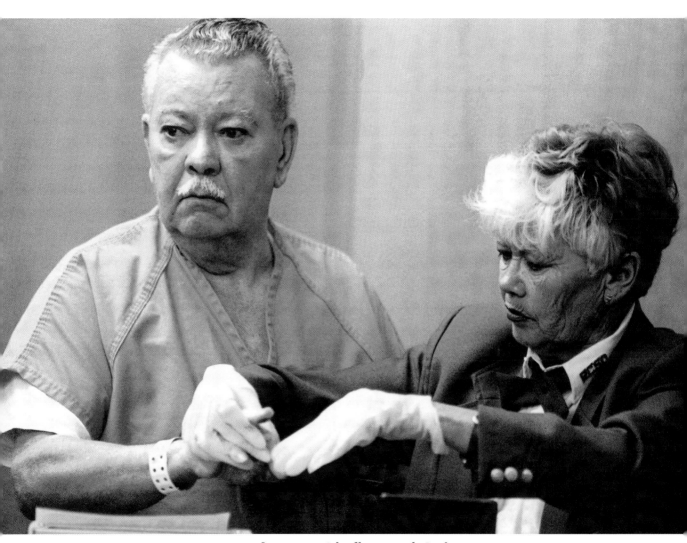

A suspect is fingerprinted.

Police Officers

The people walking around in uniforms are police officers. They are men and women who work in your community. They **patrol** the streets, parks, and alleys stopping crime.

Some police officers work all day in a station. Others drive police cars. Some officers patrol on foot, bicycle, motorcycle, or even on horseback.

You might visit the **briefing room** where orders are handed out. Police work is hard and dangerous. But police officers do their job because they want to make a difference in their community.

Opposite page:
A police officer on a horse talking with some children.

THE POLICE STATION

records room

911 CENTER

dispatch room

CHIEF

RECORDS

INFORMATION

POLICE

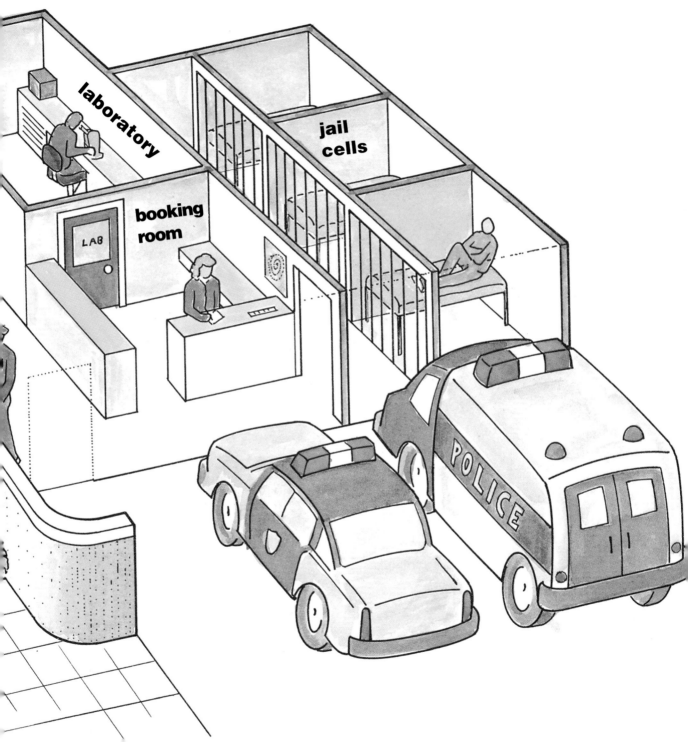

laboratory

jail
cells

booking
room

LAB

POLICE

The Police Officer's Job

Police officers do many jobs. They catch criminals. They give drivers tickets for breaking traffic laws. They rescue people who are sick or in trouble. They go to people's homes when help is needed. And police officers help people who have been in accidents.

If you ever need a police officer's help, dial 9-1-1 on your telephone.

Opposite page: Police officers are very helpful and are always willing to talk with you.

13

The Dispatch Room

Most telephone calls to the police are answered in one area of the station, the **dispatch** room. When people dial 9-1-1 for help, a dispatcher answers a call. The dispatcher sends an officer in a car to help the caller.

Large computers are kept in another room of the police station. This is where police records are kept. These records keep track of criminals and crimes that have been solved. They also list records of unsolved crimes and criminals who have not been captured.

Other areas of the police station are offices. **Detectives** and police officers work there to fill out records that are filed in the computers.

Opposite page: An officer in the dispatch room.

Suspects and Criminals

Everyone is considered **innocent** until they are proven **guilty** in a court of law. Police officers must remember those words when they arrest someone who may have broken the law. Until someone is given a **trial**, they are called **suspects**. That is because they are suspected of breaking the law.

Sometimes suspects are put in a lineup with innocent people around them. Crime victims stand behind one-way mirrors so that suspects cannot see their face. Crime victims pick the suspect from the innocent people.

When suspects are arrested, they are taken to the **booking room**. The suspects' fingers are rubbed with ink. Then they push their inky fingerprints down on a piece of paper. This is called fingerprinting a suspect. No two people have the same fingerprints. The **suspects'** fingerprints are put on the police computer to see if they can be matched with fingerprints at a **crime scene**.

After suspects are fingerprinted, they are photographed. Then they are put into a **jail cell**. Suspects may pay **bail** until a trial is held. If the crime is very serious, or the criminal might run away, bail is not allowed.

Jails in police stations are used to keep suspects for a short time. If suspects are held for a long time, they are sent to bigger jails.

Every jail looks different. Some have big rooms with iron bars that go from the floor to the ceiling. Other jails have rooms with locked doors and barred windows. Not everyone on a field trip gets to visit the jail cells.

The Police Lab

You will probably visit the police **laboratory**. The police use the lab to find clues that can help solve crimes. They lift fingerprint images from objects. And they examine hairs and fibers from **crime scenes**.

Police gather **evidence** using tools in the lab. The evidence proves that a crime happened. The evidence may link a **suspect** to a crime. This evidence is used in court to prove that a suspect is **guilty**.

**Opposite page:
An officer in the police laboratory looking for fingerprints.**

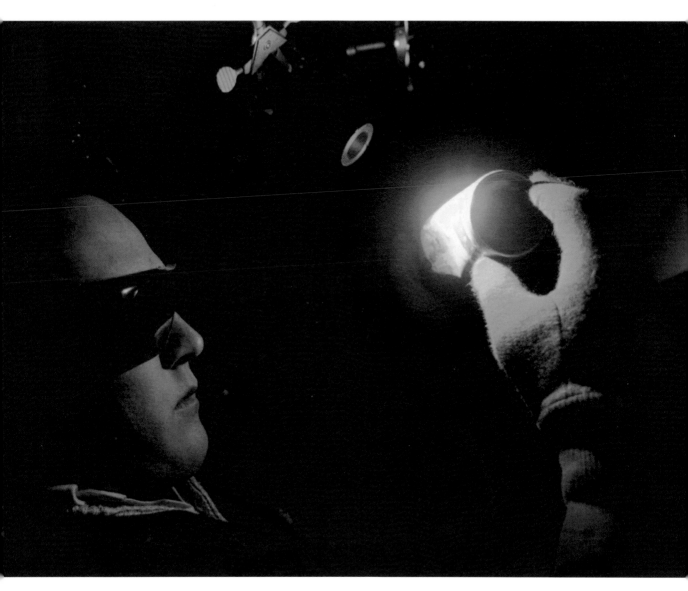

A Police Officer's Tools

Just as a carpenter needs a hammer, police officers need tools for their trade. They carry a radio so they can call other officers. They carry pistols and bullets to protect themselves. They also carry handcuffs and a club for arresting **suspects**. Some police officers wear bulletproof vests.

Police officers drive **squad** cars. The squad car has bright flashing lights and a siren. It also has a computer so officers may look at police records while on **patrol**. Squad cars also carry search and rescue equipment.

Police officers work to protect young people. When you visit a police station, say "Hello!" to an officer.

A neighborhood police officer talks with some young people.

21

Glossary

bail - the money left with the court in order to free a person from jail until the trial is held.

booking room - a room where an accusation is written down against a person in a police record.

briefing (BREE-fing) **room** - a room where police officers interview suspects for detailed information.

crime scene - an area where a crime has been committed.

detective (dee-TEK-tiv) - a police officer who does not wear a uniform, examines crime scenes, and captures suspects.

dispatcher (DISS-patch-er) - a person who works at a police station answering emergency calls. The dispatcher tells police where help is needed.

evidence (EV-uh-dents) - items used to prove a crime happened.

guilty (GILL-tee) - having committed a crime.

innocent (IN-uh-sent) - free from having done wrong.

jail cell - a small room where a criminal is detained.

laboratory (LAB-ruh-tor-ee) - a place with special equipment where scientific experiments and tests are done.

patrol - to pass through an area looking for crime.

squad (SKWAD) - a small, organized group of people.

suspect - a person who police think may have committed a crime.

trial - examining and deciding a case in court.

Index